Education Must Change

Expectations are changing…

"Today's kids think differently than we do. The speed of technological advances and the frantic pace of media delivery have changed what students expect from teachers and what they learn. To effectively reach these young people, teachers need technological tools to meet kids where they are and to engage them in school activities."

Kimberly Vidoni, PhD
Educational Technology Coordinator
Nevada Department of Education

Teaching is changing…

"We can achieve so much more if we are actively engaged in professional learning communities. Teachers are empowered to collaborate with colleagues across the hall or halfway around the world as they explore strategies for advancing student learning and inspiring creativity and innovation—one student at a time."

Trina Davis, PhD, ISTE President
Assistant Professor and
Director of eEducation
Texas A&M University

Societies are changing…

"Societies are changing into knowledge societies. Globalization has expanded opportunities around the world. Thus we may all benefit by using a common vocabulary when thinking about the future direction of teaching, learning, and leading."

Tarek Shawki
Director, UNESCO
Cairo Office

Educators Must Lead

As technologies dramatically increase their penetration into our society, teachers need to demonstrate the skills and behaviors of digital-age professionals. Competence with technology skills is the foundation. To be part of the transformation to 21st-century teaching and learning, however, teachers need to lead by modeling effective ICT skills and lifelong learning strategies. Students need to see their teachers apply the basics in authentic, integrated ways that manifest in student experience solving problems, collaborating on projects, and creatively extending their abilities. It is these kinds of experiences that will help students meet the National Educational Technology Standards for Students (NETS•S) and prepare them as future workers, leaders, and contributing global citizens.

For that reason, the ISTE National Educational Technology Standards for Teachers (NETS•T) are strongly aligned with the NETS•S. The NETS•T build on the NETS•S by adding critical professional behaviors and responsibilities that must be embraced if we are to truly improve the teaching profession. The refreshed NETS•T are meant to transform education and provide students the opportunity to learn effectively for a lifetime and live productively in our emerging global society and increasingly digital world.

Supporting a New Generation of Technology Standards

Today's economic and social landscape is changing faster than ever. Effective implementation of the NETS•S will provide the foundational knowledge and skills that are necessary for students to thrive in this changing world. Teachers who meet the NETS•T will be prepared to guide their students on an engaging, rewarding, and rich learning pathway toward meeting the NETS•S.

The essential conditions on page 3 are necessary if teachers are to successfully demonstrate their mastery of the NETS•T by creating learning environments conducive to creativity, innovation, and powerful uses of ICT.

"It is change, continuing change, inevitable change, that is the dominant factor in society today. No sensible decision can be made any longer without taking into account not only the world as it is, but the world as it will be."

Isaac Asimov

Definitions

ICT stands for information and communication technology. This acronym is used throughout much of the world in place of the word *technology* when referring to skills or standards for technology use.

Educational technology refers to the application of technology skills for learning.

Expectations Have Changed and Evolved

Teachers are expected to employ technology, as well as to demonstrate their competence using behaviours that are extensive. They are judged in terms of how much they know about instructional technology, the skills they use, and how well they apply their knowledge and skills. Thus they must demonstrate a variety of abilities in a variety of contexts. They are also expected to engage students as willing partners in technology in the classroom. Teachers are expected to integrate productivity tools with instruction and also integrate the Internet, e-mail, the use of mobile devices, educational software, and more. They are expected to create learning environments in which students are actively engaged and where students demonstrate their own competence using technology.

Kathleen A. Bowes, Antonia D'Onofrio, and Elaine S. Marker, *Assessing technology integration: Its validity and value for classroom practice and teacher accountability,* Australasian Journal of Educational Technology 2006, 22(4), 439–454

Essential Conditions

Necessary conditions to effectively leverage technology for learning

Shared Vision
Proactive leadership in developing a shared vision for educational technology among all education stakeholders including teachers and support staff, school and district administrators, teacher educators, students, parents, and the community

Empowered Leaders
Stakeholders at every level empowered to be leaders in effecting change

Implementation Planning
A systemic plan aligned with a shared vision for school effectiveness and student learning through the infusion of information and communication technologies (ICT) and digital learning resources

Consistent and Adequate Funding
Ongoing funding to support technology infrastructure, personnel, digital resources, and staff development

Equitable Access
Robust and reliable access to current and emerging technologies and digital resources, with connectivity for all students, teachers, staff, and school leaders

Skilled Personnel
Educators, support staff, and other leaders skilled in the selection and effective use of appropriate ICT resources

Ongoing Professional Learning
Technology-related professional learning plans and opportunities with dedicated time to practice and share ideas

Technical Support
Consistent and reliable assistance for maintaining, renewing, and using ICT and digital learning resources

Curriculum Framework
Content standards and related digital curriculum resources that are aligned with and support digital-age learning and work

Student-Centered Learning
Planning, teaching, and assessment centered around the needs and abilities of students

Assessment and Evaluation
Continuous assessment, both of learning and for learning, and evaluation of the use of ICT and digital resources

Engaged Communities
Partnerships and collaboration within communities to support and fund the use of ICT and digital learning resources

Support Policies
Policies, financial plans, accountability measures, and incentive structures to support the use of ICT and other digital resources for learning and in district school operations

Supportive External Context
Policies and initiatives at the national, regional, and local levels to support schools and teacher preparation programs in the effective implementation of technology for achieving curriculum and learning technology (ICT) standards

Teachers Transform Learning Environments!

Today's teachers must be responsible for providing a learning environment that takes students beyond the walls of their classrooms and into a world of endless opportunities through effective infusion of relevant content with up-to-date and emerging tools and resources. This classroom transformation is imperative in ensuring digital-age students are empowered to learn, live, and work successfully, today and tomorrow!

Transforming Learning Environments with Technology
Technology-Enabled Strategies for Student Learning

Traditional Environments	→ Emerging Learning Landscape
Teacher-directed, memory-focused instruction	Student-centered, performance-focused learning
Lockstep, prescribed-path progression	Flexible progression with multipath options
Limited media, single-sense stimulation	Media-rich, multisensory stimulation
Knowledge from limited, authoritative sources	Learner-constructed knowledge from multiple information sources and experiences
Isolated work on invented exercises	Collaborative work on authentic, real-world projects
Mastery of fixed content and specified processes	Student engagement in definition, design, and management of projects
Factual, literal thinking for competence	Creative thinking for innovation and original solutions
In-school expertise, content, and activities	Global expertise, information, and learning experiences
Stand-alone communication and information tools	Converging information and communication systems
Traditional literacy and communication skills	Digital literacies and communication skills
Primary focus on school and local community	Expanded focus including digital global citizenship
Isolated assessment of learning	Integrated assessment for learning

Students and Teachers
Technology Standards for the Digital-Age Classroom

ISTE NETS for Students

Creativity and Innovation

Communication and Collaboration

Research and Information Fluency

Critical Thinking, Problem Solving, and Decision Making

Digital Citizenship

Technology Operations and Concepts

ISTE NETS for Teachers

Facilitate and Inspire Student Learning and Creativity

Design and Develop Digital-Age Learning Experiences and Assessments

Model Digital-Age Work and Learning

Promote and Model Digital Citizenship and Responsibility

Engage in Professional Growth and Leadership

Adapting the Refreshed NETS•T for Global Use

Regardless of where you live, advances in technology are having an effect on your life. In places where access is still a burning issue, you are probably trying to identify ways to develop and launch a reliable infrastructure so that students and teachers may begin mastering basic technology skills. In places where infrastructure is no longer a concern, you are most likely grappling with how to give your students a competitive edge in this new global society and how to educate teachers about technology and its potential for improving student learning. In any case, the NETS•T may be adapted to help meet your educational needs. An additional resource that complements the refreshed NETS•T benchmarks is UNESCO's ICT Competency Framework for Teachers, which serves to build a common vocabulary for ICT and promotes professional development and policy requirements to implement effective ICT integration. Here are a few steps you can take to get started:

1. Secure the support of essential stakeholders.

2. If you don't have existing technology (ICT) standards and technology is not incorporated into your content standards, follow the process outlined in the *National Educational Technology Standards for Students, Second Edition* (ISTE, 2007) on adapting the refreshed NETS•S for global use.

3. If you don't have existing technology (ICT) standards for teachers or if technology is not incorporated into your teaching standards, use the ISTE NETS•T as a foundation.

4. If you already have national technology standards for teachers or subject area teaching standards that incorporate technology, compare them with the ISTE NETS•T to identify gaps.

5. Review your teaching standards to identify opportunities for integration with the ISTE NETS•T or to determine if all the NETS•T have been addressed.

6. Review the scenarios found in the Rubrics section of this booklet and gather your own examples of exemplary technology use on the part of teachers and students.

7. Use local experts from within your own community or country who support instructional technology use.

8. When it is time to localize the NETS•T, you will need adequate resources to:

   a. obtain accurate translations of the standards and profiles,

   b. put them into the context of your culture, and

   c. address the needs of your teachers and students in a process that builds consensus among all stakeholders.

What students should know and be able to do to learn effectively and live productively in an increasingly digital world...

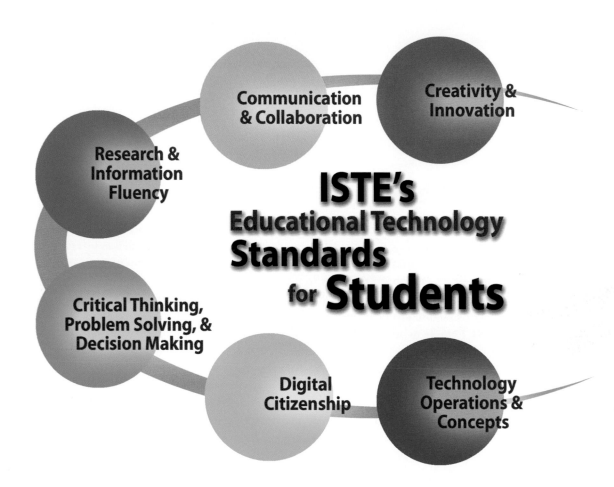

NETS•S Organization

The technology standards for students are divided into six broad categories. A brief standard statement follows each category. The four performance indicators (a–d) for each standard provide specific outcomes to be measured.

The ISTE
National Educational Technology Standards (NETS•S) and Performance Indicators for Students

1. **Creativity and Innovation**

   Students demonstrate creative thinking, construct knowledge, and develop innovative products and processes using technology. Students:
     a. apply existing knowledge to generate new ideas, products, or processes
     b. create original works as a means of personal or group expression
     c. use models and simulations to explore complex systems and issues
     d. identify trends and forecast possibilities

2. **Communication and Collaboration**

   Students use digital media and environments to communicate and work collaboratively, including at a distance, to support individual learning and contribute to the learning of others. Students:
     a. interact, collaborate, and publish with peers, experts, or others employing a variety of digital environments and media
     b. communicate information and ideas effectively to multiple audiences using a variety of media and formats
     c. develop cultural understanding and global awareness by engaging with learners of other cultures
     d. contribute to project teams to produce original works or solve problems

3. **Research and Information Fluency**

   Students apply digital tools to gather, evaluate, and use information. Students:
     a. plan strategies to guide inquiry
     b. locate, organize, analyze, evaluate, synthesize, and ethically use information from a variety of sources and media
     c. evaluate and select information sources and digital tools based on the appropriateness to specific tasks
     d. process data and report results

4. **Critical Thinking, Problem Solving, and Decision Making**

   Students use critical thinking skills to plan and conduct research, manage projects, solve problems, and make informed decisions using appropriate digital tools and resources. Students:
     a. identify and define authentic problems and significant questions for investigation
     b. plan and manage activities to develop a solution or complete a project
     c. collect and analyze data to identify solutions and/or make informed decisions
     d. use multiple processes and diverse perspectives to explore alternative solutions

5. **Digital Citizenship**

   Students understand human, cultural, and societal issues related to technology and practice legal and ethical behavior. Students:
     a. advocate and practice safe, legal, and responsible use of information and technology
     b. exhibit a positive attitude toward using technology that supports collaboration, learning, and productivity
     c. demonstrate personal responsibility for lifelong learning
     d. exhibit leadership for digital citizenship

6. **Technology Operations and Concepts**

   Students demonstrate a sound understanding of technology concepts, systems, and operations. Students:
     a. understand and use technology systems
     b. select and use applications effectively and productively
     c. troubleshoot systems and applications
     d. transfer current knowledge to learning of new technologies

What teachers should know and be able to apply to teach effectively and grow professionally in an increasingly digital world...

Student Learning & Creativity

Digital-Age Learning Experiences & Assessments

ISTE's Educational Technology Standards for Teachers

Digital-Age Work & Learning

Professional Growth & Leadership

Digital Citizenship & Responsibility

NETS•T Organization

The technology standards for teachers are organized into five broad categories. A brief standard statement follows each category. The four performance indicators (a–d) for each standard provide specific outcomes to be measured. The Rubrics and Scenarios for Digital-Age Teachers (see pp. 10–21) provide examples of teacher performances at various growth and professional levels.

The ISTE
National Educational Technology Standards (NETS•T) and Performance Indicators for Teachers

Effective teachers model and apply the National Educational Technology Standards for Students (NETS•S) as they design, implement, and assess learning experiences to engage students and improve learning; enrich professional practice; and provide positive models for students, colleagues, and the community. All teachers should meet the following standards and performance indicators. Teachers:

1. Facilitate and Inspire Student Learning and Creativity

Teachers use their knowledge of subject matter, teaching and learning, and technology to facilitate experiences that advance student learning, creativity, and innovation in both face-to-face and virtual environments. Teachers:

- **a.** promote, support, and model creative and innovative thinking and inventiveness
- **b.** engage students in exploring real-world issues and solving authentic problems using digital tools and resources
- **c.** promote student reflection using collaborative tools to reveal and clarify students' conceptual understanding and thinking, planning, and creative processes
- **d.** model collaborative knowledge construction by engaging in learning with students, colleagues, and others in face-to-face and virtual environments

2. Design and Develop Digital-Age Learning Experiences and Assessments

Teachers design, develop, and evaluate authentic learning experiences and assessments incorporating contemporary tools and resources to maximize content learning in context and to develop the knowledge, skills, and attitudes identified in the NETS•S. Teachers:

- **a.** design or adapt relevant learning experiences that incorporate digital tools and resources to promote student learning and creativity
- **b.** develop technology-enriched learning environments that enable all students to pursue their individual curiosities and become active participants in setting their own educational goals, managing their own learning, and assessing their own progress
- **c.** customize and personalize learning activities to address students' diverse learning styles, working strategies, and abilities using digital tools and resources
- **d.** provide students with multiple and varied formative and summative assessments aligned with content and technology standards and use resulting data to inform learning and teaching

3. Model Digital-Age Work and Learning

Teachers exhibit knowledge, skills, and work processes representative of an innovative professional in a global and digital society. Teachers:

- **a.** demonstrate fluency in technology systems and the transfer of current knowledge to new technologies and situations
- **b.** collaborate with students, peers, parents, and community members using digital tools and resources to support student success and innovation
- **c.** communicate relevant information and ideas effectively to students, parents, and peers using a variety of digital-age media and formats
- **d.** model and facilitate effective use of current and emerging digital tools to locate, analyze, evaluate, and use information resources to support research and learning

4. Promote and Model Digital Citizenship and Responsibility

Teachers understand local and global societal issues and responsibilities in an evolving digital culture and exhibit legal and ethical behavior in their professional practices. Teachers:

- **a.** advocate, model, and teach safe, legal, and ethical use of digital information and technology, including respect for copyright, intellectual property, and the appropriate documentation of sources
- **b.** address the diverse needs of all learners by using learner-centered strategies and providing equitable access to appropriate digital tools and resources
- **c.** promote and model digital etiquette and responsible social interactions related to the use of technology and information
- **d.** develop and model cultural understanding and global awareness by engaging with colleagues and students of other cultures using digital-age communication and collaboration tools

5. Engage in Professional Growth and Leadership

Teachers continuously improve their professional practice, model lifelong learning, and exhibit leadership in their school and professional community by promoting and demonstrating the effective use of digital tools and resources. Teachers:

- **a.** participate in local and global learning communities to explore creative applications of technology to improve student learning
- **b.** exhibit leadership by demonstrating a vision of technology infusion, participating in shared decision making and community building, and developing the leadership and technology skills of others
- **c.** evaluate and reflect on current research and professional practice on a regular basis to make effective use of existing and emerging digital tools and resources in support of student learning
- **d.** contribute to the effectiveness, vitality, and self-renewal of the teaching profession and of their school and community

Rubrics and Scenarios
for Digital-Age Teachers

Additional components of the NETS Project include rubrics describing key performance benchmarks for the use of technology as a tool for teaching and learning and scenarios describing authentic classroom activities illustrating ways the standards, indicators, and rubrics can be addressed in practice. It is ISTE's belief that all teachers must strive to help transition schools from industrial-age to digital-age places of learning. Along with the standards, the rubrics and scenarios provide tools to help teachers successfully make this transition.

Rubrics

The rubrics are intended to provide examples of performance criteria at increasing levels of attainment that may be used to identify the success of teachers and teacher candidates in the full implementation of each standard:

- The Beginning Level describes behaviors expected of candidates in teacher education programs or practicing teachers who are just beginning to use technology to improve teaching and learning.

- The Developing Level describes behaviors expected of teachers who are becoming more adept and flexible in their use of technology in an educational setting.

- The Proficient Level describes behaviors indicating that teachers are using technology efficiently and effectively for improving student learning.

- The Transformative Level describes behaviors that involve exploring, adapting, and applying technology in ways that fundamentally change teaching and learning and address the needs of an increasingly global and digital society.

The rubrics are based on criteria (or descriptors) of performance at the described levels rather than on artificial age ranges, teacher preparation levels, or years of service. Therefore, whether these rubrics are used in conjunction with professional development of classroom teachers or are used with teacher candidates in their field experiences, practica, student teaching, or internships in PK–12 (ages 5–adult) classrooms, the same rubrics can be used to assess growth in use of the NETS for Teachers.

Additionally, these sets of rubrics are models that can be modified or expanded to meet national, state/province, district, school, teacher preparation, or other program needs. They are designed by ISTE to facilitate the understanding of and the levels of success related to each standard.

It is important to remember that the rubric descriptors are indicators of achievement at certain stages in a teacher's mastery of the standards. Success in meeting the indicators is predicated on teachers having regular access to a system of support as described in the essential conditions (see p. 3). Without such a support system in place, it is very difficult for teachers to reach the Transformative Level of implementation.

Scenarios

The scenarios that accompany the rubrics describe authentic activities in which teachers are using technology to increase skills and expand or enhance learning in the classroom. The activities describe educators who are working at the Proficient Level of the rubric and include a sidebar describing next steps to reach the Transformative Level. The activities also reflect the NETS•T and performance indicators within the context of relevant content-based activities, underscoring a core belief at ISTE that technology use should not occur in isolation but as an integral tool for teaching and learning across all skills and subject areas.

The activities described in the rubrics and scenarios are examples only, not a definitive list of activities required to meet a standard/indicator. There are many different activities and scenarios that could demonstrate achievement of the ISTE NETS for Teachers.

Rubric for Student Learning & Creativity

1. Facilitate and Inspire Student Learning and Creativity

Teachers use their knowledge of subject matter, teaching and learning, and technology to facilitate experiences that advance student learning, creativity, and innovation in both face-to-face and virtual environments. Teachers:

Performance Indicator	Beginning	Developing	Proficient	Transformative
a. promote, support, and model creative and innovative thinking and inventiveness	research and discuss ways students can use digital tools and resources to enhance creative and innovative thinking and to develop and express their understandings of knowledge and concepts.	facilitate creative thinking and inventiveness by modeling thought processes and creating visual representations of concept development and problem solving.	enable students to demonstrate creative thinking, construct knowledge, and develop innovative products and processes by promoting and supporting these activities and modeling related knowledge, skills, and attitudes.	regularly engage with students as lead learner in creative thinking activities and inspire students to explore complex issues, generate new ideas, create and critique original works, and develop and evaluate new products and processes.
b. engage students in exploring real-world issues and solving authentic problems using digital tools and resources	develop technology-based learning activities to engage students in critical thinking, creativity, and authentic problem solving centered on real-world issues.	involve students in researching real-world problems and issues and evaluating diverse solutions using digital tools and resources.	facilitate activities that engage students in planning and managing research projects focused on real-world issues, in applying critical thinking to solve authentic problems, and in selecting appropriate digital tools and resources to accomplish and enhance the process.	regularly involve students in learning experiences that require identifying and defining authentic questions and problems, planning for and managing their research, and using multiple processes and perspectives to discover, propose, and evaluate multiple solutions.
c. promote student reflection using collaborative tools to reveal and clarify students' conceptual understanding and thinking, planning, and creative processes	demonstrate the use of collaborative tools to promote student reflection, planning, and creative thinking.	facilitate and support student use of collaborative tools to reflect on and clarify their own thinking, planning, and creativity.	engage students in reflecting on and clarifying their own thinking, planning, and creative processes, in correcting misconceptions, and in using meta-cognitive thinking strategies with collaborative tools and environments.	involve students in ongoing examination and evaluation of their own thinking, planning, and creativity. Encourage learners to articulate and share their thinking with others through technology-enhanced team work.
d. model collaborative knowledge construction by engaging in learning with students, colleagues, and others in face-to-face and virtual environments	research and identify strategies for facilitating knowledge construction and creative thinking in either face-to-face or virtual environments.	facilitate knowledge construction, creative thinking, and collaborative interaction by engaging in learning with students, colleagues, and others in either face-to-face or virtual environments.	model knowledge construction and creative thinking by working collaboratively with individuals and groups, contributing to learning both face-to-face and virtually.	model knowledge construction and creative thinking in a variety of face-to-face and virtual learning environments and situations by engaging in real-world problem solving with students, peers, and experts.

Scenario for Student Learning & Creativity

1.   Facilitate and Inspire Student Learning and Creativity

Performance Indicator 1.c   Promote student reflection using collaborative tools to reveal and clarify students' conceptual understanding and thinking, planning, and creative processes.

Other NETS Alignments   NETS•T 1.a, b; 2.a; NETS•S 1.a, b; 2.a; 3.d; 6.a

Proficient Level Rubric   Engage students in reflecting on and clarifying their own thinking, planning, and creative processes, in correcting misconceptions, and in using meta-cognitive thinking strategies with collaborative tools and environments.

Walk into any of Maria Dayton's secondary school social studies classes and you'll find that all her students, whether working individually or in pairs, are deeply engaged in the tasks at hand. And, if you ask students to explain what they're doing, be prepared for detailed responses that include a description of their thinking processes. How did Dayton create this rich learning environment?

Not long ago, Dayton was increasingly troubled by the fact that her students reported getting most of their information about international events and their underlying factors via brief postings on blogs and online news resources. "It's not that they were necessarily getting misinformation," she explains, "My concerns were rooted in the fact that I didn't see students taking the time to think about what they read and heard or to use the information in any meaningful way." As a result, class discussions and presentations were nearly always at a very superficial level.

Then Dayton attended a workshop on using technology to support meta-cognitive thinking strategies offered by the school's librarian. Dayton frequently asked her students to write reflections about work they'd completed, but that was as far as it went. The strategies the librarian described sounded like they might address her concerns.

> ### Taking It to the Transformative Level
>
> *Involve students in ongoing examination and evaluation of their own thinking, planning, and creativity. Encourage learners to articulate and share their thinking with others through technology-enhanced team work.*
>
> *Dayton's students are required to complete a year-long project. In the past, she has established the schedule and led students through each phase of the project. Now she plans to turn responsibility for project management over to the students. Using a Web-based group organizer, student teams will estimate time requirements, establish a schedule, and track task completion. Teams will use a social bookmarking Web service to share online resources and applications to work collaboratively on preparing and sharing their final projects.*

Today, Dayton's students grapple daily with "thinking about their thinking." For example, when beginning a new instructional unit, students build on previous knowledge by identifying what they already know and what they want to learn using Web-based, collaborative concept-mapping tools. They return to these initial concept maps throughout the unit to clarify, expand, or sometimes replace their initial statements.

Dayton encourages students to pair up as they work to understand concepts presented in lessons and through their reading. As one student talks through the material, explaining his thinking about the information, the other listens, asking clarifying questions. In-class discussions happen face to face, but after school students make phone calls over the Internet to conduct and record their discussions. These conversations also form the basis for reciprocal teaching opportunities where students use a document camera and notes or project documents created using Web-based applications to share information, ask questions, or summarize the material being studied.

Dayton says her next step is to expand these strategies into a year-long project where students will take responsibility for planning every aspect of the project.

Rubric for Digital-Age Learning Experiences & Assessments

2. Design and Develop Digital-Age Learning Experiences and Assessments

Teachers design, develop, and evaluate authentic learning experiences and assessments incorporating contemporary tools and resources to maximize content learning in context and to develop the knowledge, skills, and attitudes identified in the NETS•S. Teachers:

Performance Indicator	Beginning	Developing	Proficient	Transformative
a. design or adapt relevant learning experiences that incorporate digital tools and resources to promote student learning and creativity	explain how existing learning resources could be designed or adapted to include students' use of technology tools to research and collect information online and to create a digital product.	adapt or create learning experiences that include students' use of technology tools to research and collect information online and to create a report, presentation, or other product.	design and customize technology-enriched learning experiences that engage students in developing research questions about real-world issues or problems, proposing and evaluating multiple creative solutions, and presenting a report to an audience, either face-to-face or virtually, for feedback.	engage students in collaborative learning challenges where they research global problems. Guide learners to select a specific problem to investigate, create research questions, select and employ strategies, and determine best solutions. Students use technology tools to present their results and share information for application in a real-world setting.
b. develop technology-enriched learning environments that enable all students to pursue their individual curiosities and become active participants in setting their own educational goals, managing their own learning, and assessing their own progress	research and discuss ways in which technology resources enable students to explore questions and issues of individual interest and to plan and manage related research.	select and demonstrate the use of technology resources that enable students to explore questions and issues of individual interest and to plan, manage, and assess their own learning.	facilitate the use of technology resources to enable students to pursue questions and issues of individual interest, to identify and manage learning goals, to record reflections, and to assess their progress and outcomes.	enable students to independently use technology resources to manage their own learning goals, plan learning strategies, and evaluate their progress and outcomes.
c. customize and personalize learning activities to address students' diverse learning styles, working strategies, and abilities using digital tools and resources	research and design learning activities that use digital tools and resources to address a variety of learning styles, work strategies, abilities, and developmental levels.	customize technology-based materials to address the learning styles, work strategies, abilities, and developmental levels of individual students.	facilitate student learning by recognizing preferred learning styles, work strategies, abilities, and developmental levels of students. Develop and use specific strategies that incorporate digital tools and resources to effectively differentiate learning experiences.	identify and develop with students personalized learning experiences aligned with preferred learning styles, work strategies, and abilities.
d. provide students with multiple and varied formative and summative assessments aligned with content and technology standards and use resulting data to inform learning and teaching	select examples of technology-based formative and summative assessments and demonstrate how they can be used to inform learning and teaching.	develop and conduct technology-based formative and summative assessments to inform learning and teaching.	provide students with multiple and varied opportunities to demonstrate their learning, and make data-based decisions to customize and adapt future learning opportunities aligned with content and technology standards.	engage students in the development and analysis of formative and summative assessments to adjust teaching and learning for increased success.

Scenario for Digital-Age Learning Experiences & Assessments

2. Design and Develop Digital-Age Learning Experiences and Assessments

Performance Indicator 2.a	Design or adapt relevant learning experiences that incorporate digital tools and resources to promote student learning and creativity.
Other NETS Alignments	NETS•T 1.a, b; 3.d; NETS•S 1.a, b; 3.c, d; 4.a, b, c; 6.a, b
Proficient Level Rubric	Design and customize technology-enriched learning experiences that engage students in developing research questions about real-world issues or problems, proposing and evaluating multiple creative solutions, and presenting a report to an audience, either face-to-face or virtually, for feedback.

Third-year teacher Amrit Narayan works with six year olds. Each morning begins with a series of calendar- and weather-related activities, where students record the temperature and weather conditions for the day. Narayan's students use a probe connected to a PDA to measure the temperature in degrees Celsius. Eleven-year-old class buddies help students use a Web-based graphing tool to generate weekly charts showing changes in temperature and weather over time.

One spring morning, a student asked why he felt cooler when he wore a white shirt on a warm day. Narayan immediately decided to turn this teachable moment into the class project for the upcoming science fair. Using a concept-mapping tool to create a brainstorming document that he projected for the children to see as they talked, students helped Narayan formulate a research question for the project: How does the color of my clothing affect how comfortable I am on a hot day?

Narayan created an online class science journal that he projected during discussions. Then, with the help of the class buddies, students took turns entering notes and data into this document. Narayan asked the students how they would design an experiment to answer their question. They decided to begin with a list of their favorite colors. This list (white, pink, yellow, green, blue, and black) was added to the online journal. Next, students predicted which colors would be most comfortable on a hot day, entering the predictions into their online graphing tool. This led to the following class hypothesis: If I wear light-colored clothing on a hot day, I will be more comfortable than if I wear dark-colored clothing.

> ### Taking It to the Transformative Level
>
> *Engage students in collaborative learning challenges where they research global problems. Guide learners to select a specific problem to investigate, create research questions, select and employ strategies, and determine best solutions. Students use technology tools to present their results and share information for application in a real-world setting.*
>
> *Now that Narayan's students understand the relationship between the color of their clothing and how comfortable they are on a hot day, they can apply that knowledge to other real-world questions. There are a variety of free tools his students can use to work collaboratively and then report their findings to a wide audience.*

The actual experiment required more thinking. After much discussion, Narayan suggested using colored construction paper to make one envelope for each color on the list. By slipping the temperature probe into each envelope, students could measure and record the temperature, leave the envelopes in the sun for a specific time, then check and record the temperature again.

After five days, students used the Web-based graphing tool to create and analyze charts that showed their hypothesis was correct. Working with the class buddies, Narayan's students created an online media album presentation to explain the class project from start to finish. Best of all, each student was able to contribute to the narration, which was broadcast during the science fair.

Rubric for Digital-Age Work & Learning

3. Model Digital-Age Work and Learning

Teachers exhibit knowledge, skills, and work processes representative of an innovative professional in a global and digital society. Teachers:

Performance Indicator	Beginning	Developing	Proficient	Transformative
a. demonstrate fluency in technology systems and the transfer of current knowledge to new technologies and situations	select and use hardware and software best suited to particular learning experiences and plan student learning experiences that appropriately use these tools.	plan, manage, and facilitate students' understanding and use of hardware and software best suited to particular learning experiences.	demonstrate and model efficient and effective use of a variety of digital tools and resources, select tools and systems best suited to accomplish teaching, learning, and assessment activities, and transfer this knowledge to new technologies and situations.	engage with students in collaborative exploration of emerging technologies and investigate together how these tools can be used in real world situations to solve problems. Involve students in identifying and solving common hardware and software problems that occur in everyday use.
b. collaborate with students, peers, parents, and community members using digital tools and resources to support student success and innovation	explore and demonstrate digital tools and resources for communicating and collaborating with students and other stakeholders to share information and establish a connection between school and home environments.	communicate and collaborate with students and other stakeholders to share information and to support creativity, innovation, and improved learning outcomes.	effectively communicate and collaborate with students, peers, parents, and community members using a variety of digital tools to support student learning, problem solving, and the production of original works.	employ a variety of digital environments and media to collaborate with project teams or learners of other countries and cultures to produce original works or solve shared problems.
c. communicate relevant information and ideas effectively to students, parents, and peers using a variety of digital-age media and formats	research and demonstrate effective use of digital resources for communicating with students, parents, and peers.	communicate relevant information and ideas to students, parents, and peers using multiple digital media and formats.	select and use the most relevant, facilitative, and effective media for communicating specific types of information and ideas to students, parents, and peers.	evaluate and use a variety of digital tools, resources, and media to communicate information and ideas to a global audience, demonstrating cultural understanding.
d. model and facilitate effective use of current and emerging digital tools to locate, analyze, evaluate, and use information resources to support research and learning	identify and discuss the effective use of current and emerging tools and resources to locate, analyze, evaluate, and use information resources for research and learning.	demonstrate the use of current digital tools to locate, analyze, evaluate, and apply information resources to support and disseminate student research and learning strategies.	model and facilitate effective use of current and emerging digital tools and resources to locate, analyze, evaluate and use information resources to support research and learning for themselves and for students.	use current and emerging digital tools and resources efficiently and effectively to deepen knowledge of information fluency and its application to teaching and learning and share results with students, parents, and colleagues.

Scenario for Digital-Age Work & Learning

3. Model Digital-Age Work and Learning

Performance Indicator 3.c	Communicate relevant information and ideas effectively to students, parents, and peers using a variety of digital-age media and formats.
Other NETS Alignments	NETS•T 1.c; 3.d; 4.c; NETS•S 2.a, c; 5.a, b
Proficient Level Rubric	Select and use the most relevant, facilitative, and effective media for communicating specific types of information and ideas to students, parents, and peers.

Miles Rockwell is a veteran secondary school teacher. Student and parent communication is extremely important to him, and he has faithfully used the school's automated homework hotline and teacher voicemail system to keep families informed.

The district implemented a Learning Management System (LMS) two years ago. Rockwell initially viewed the LMS as a fancy attendance automation system, but quickly discovered there was much more to it. He attended a workshop where he learned how to set up a public Web page to share classroom information with students and parents. Families had been coaxing him to get online, and this easy-to-use system made it possible.

Next, he discovered that there were tools available for use in private areas—places where he'd want to limit access to students and parents. For example, students could take online quizzes that would be scored and recorded immediately by the system. Parents and students could access these grades within minutes! Speaking of grades, it was also possible for Rockwell's students to turn in all their assignments via the LMS. He could download them and repost graded work, and the system would update his online grade book and notify students and parents to check the results.

> ### Taking It to the Transformative Level
> *Evaluate and use a variety of digital tools, resources, and media to communicate information and ideas to a global audience, demonstrating cultural understanding.*
>
> *Rockwell and one of his colleagues plan to expand student use of the LMS to include the blog and wiki features. Their hope is to pilot several cross-curricular activities and then explore strategies for taking a required service learning project online with another school in the district. They are also investigating the feasibility of participating in one of the many online international projects available.*

Although it takes time to post homework assignments and class news on the Web page, Rockwell estimates that it's no more time than he spent updating messages on the homework hotline, creating a weekly class newsletter, and returning phone calls. And, rather than leaving voicemail, parents now e-mail questions to Rockwell.

"That part has been a bit tricky," confesses Rockwell. "At first, I was checking e-mail four or five time each day to make sure I responded quickly. Now I have an automated response that parents receive. It explains that I check and answer e-mail once each day, right after school. It also asks them to call the office directly if it's an emergency that needs a quicker response. Since adding the automated response, the e-mail part runs smoothly, too."

Rockwell and fellow department members are also using the LMS to handle routine administrative tasks. In addition to attendance, teachers now use the LMS blog feature to discuss management items that used to devour meeting time. Now, when they get together, teachers are able to focus on instructional issues.

Rubric for Digital Citizenship & Responsibility

4. Promote and Model Digital Citizenship and Responsibility

Teachers understand local and global societal issues and responsibilities in an evolving digital culture and exhibit legal and ethical behavior in their professional practices. Teachers:

Performance Indicator	Beginning	Developing	Proficient	Transformative
a. advocate, model, and teach safe, legal, and ethical use of digital information and technology, including respect for copyright, intellectual property, and the appropriate documentation of sources	research and apply effective practices for the safe, ethical, legal and healthy use of technology and the responsible care and handling of hardware, software, and information resources.	model acceptable use policies for technology resources including strategies for addressing threats to security of technology systems, data, and information.	advocate, model, and teach safe, legal, and ethical use of technology and information, including copyright, privacy issues, and cyberbullying, and security of systems, data, and information.	engage students in developing a system for promoting and monitoring safe, legal, and ethical use of digital information and technology and for determining a system for addressing misuse of technology resources.
b. address the diverse needs of all learners by using learner-centered strategies and providing equitable access to appropriate digital tools and resources.	investigate issues related to equitable access and develop strategies for managing technology to address students' diverse learning styles and developmental levels.	apply strategies to address the diverse needs of learners, including access to hardware, curriculum software, and online resources.	facilitate equitable access to digital tools and resources, use learner-centered strategies, and employ features of universal access and assistive technologies to meet the diverse needs of learners.	examine and research issues related to equitable access to technology in school, community, and home environments including identification and use of assistive technologies to meet the diverse needs of students.
c. promote and model digital etiquette and responsible social interactions related to the use of technology and information	demonstrate digital etiquette and identify how social interactions can support student learning and responsible use of technology.	model correct and careful use of digital resources and inform learners of consequences for misuse.	promote proper use of digital technology, and discuss ethical issues, digital etiquette, and real-world examples of appropriate and inappropriate uses of digital tools and resources.	engage learners in researching the responsibilities related to the use of digital tools and resources and the consequences of misuse in a global information society. Work collaboratively with students in the development of policies and procedures for responsible use of technology and information resources.
d. develop and model cultural understanding and global awareness by engaging with colleagues and students of other cultures using digital-age communication and collaboration tools	demonstrate the use of communication and collaboration tools for developing students' awareness of various cultures.	provide opportunities for students to apply communications technology resources to interact with students or experts from other communities and other countries.	involve students in opportunities to develop cultural understanding and global awareness through digital-age communications and collaboration projects with students from other countries.	engage students in collaborative research and publication with students and experts from other countries to develop global cultural understanding.

Scenario for Digital Citizenship & Responsibility

4. Promote and Model Digital Citizenship and Responsibility

Performance Indicator 4.c   Promote and model digital etiquette and responsible social interactions related to the use of technology and information.

Other NETS Alignments   NETS•T 3.b; 5.a, c; NETS•S 4.a; 5.a, d

Proficient Level Rubric   Promote proper use of digital technology, and discuss ethical issues, digital etiquette, and real-world examples of appropriate and inappropriate uses of digital tools and resources.

While on her way to her car one afternoon, first-year teacher Anneka Taggart discovered one of her 10-year-old students on the playground sobbing inconsolably. It took time to draw out the story, but Taggart learned that the student and her best friend were the targets of a cyberbullying campaign launched by other students in Taggart's class.

"And you can't do anything about it, because it happens away from school," explained the girl. "We get text messages, instant messages, there's even a blog about us where other kids write mean things. Everybody knows they can't do it at school, but home is different."

This last remark caught Taggart completely off guard. She stopped by the principal's office and explained the situation. "What can we do?" she asked.

The principal explained there were steps she would take to handle the immediate situation. "But we shouldn't stop there," she said. "It's obvious that the students understand our expectations for use of digital technology at school, but we need to help them see that proper, ethical use applies away from school, too. How would you feel about helping to find a solution?"

> ### Taking It to the Transformative Level
>
> *Engage learners in researching the responsibilities related to the use of digital tools and resources and the consequences of misuse in a global information society. Work collaboratively with students in the development of policies and procedures for responsible use of technology and information resources.*
>
> *In researching information about cyberbullying, Taggart learned that this is a global problem. Her students have volunteered to make a list of the top ten most critical scenarios on their wiki and work with her to compile their solutions to the selected scenarios. They plan to publish a handbook that will be posted on the school's Web site and offered to cyberbullying sites around the world.*

Taggart agreed. A small committee was formed, and students were surveyed about their online experiences at and away from school. No students reported being approached online by a stranger, and all said they knew not to divulge private information online. However, students reported being both victims and perpetrators of cyberbullying. And they admitted ignoring copyright law away from school, especially when downloading music and video files. A review of the online safety lessons currently taught at the school showed they were heavy on "stranger danger" but did not deal with digital problems between friends or copyright laws and downloading files.

Taggart proposed creating a series of scenarios depicting positive and detrimental situations based on students' actual experiences. These scenarios would target issues not currently addressed and could be used for classroom and online discussions with students and their parents. She created a wiki and invited students to anonymously post their greatest concerns about misuse of technology at school and at home as well as positive aspects of technology use. Committee members wrote scenarios using this information.

Now students and teachers use a growing collection of scenarios to regularly discuss and resolve critical, real-world technology-related issues.

Rubric for Professional Growth & Leadership

5. Engage in Professional Growth and Leadership

Teachers continuously improve their professional practice, model lifelong learning, and exhibit leadership in their school and professional community by promoting and demonstrating the effective use of digital tools and resources. Teachers:

Performance indicator	Beginning	Developing	Proficient	Transformative
a. participate in local and global learning communities to explore creative applications of technology to improve student learning	explore and discuss attributes of local and global learning communities where teachers can explore creative applications of technology to improve student learning.	develop plans for using local or global learning communities to explore creative applications of technology that improve student learning.	actively participate in local and global learning communities to exchange and implement ideas and methods related to creative applications of technology to improve student learning.	help develop and sustain local and global learning communities to exchange ideas and methods related to creative applications of technology and to enhance the effective use of technology for learning.
b. exhibit leadership by demonstrating a vision of technology infusion, participating in shared decision making and community building, and developing the leadership and technology skills of others	identify and evaluate local and global visions of technology infusion, ways of participating in shared decision making and community building, and strategies for developing the technology skills of others.	demonstrate leadership for implementation of the school/district vision for technology infusion by applying it in their own learning environment.	adopt a shared vision of technology infusion appropriate for the educational environment, work cooperatively with others in decision making, and contribute to the development of leadership and technology skills in others.	participate in developing a vision for technology infusion in the school and the wider community, advocate for its adoption, help facilitate shared decision making, and promote the development of leadership and technology skills in others.
c. evaluate and reflect on current research and professional practice on a regular basis to make effective use of existing and emerging digital tools and resources in support of student learning	investigate and reflect on research and professional practice for using digital tools and resources to support student learning needs.	develop technology-based learning plans that integrate current research and promising professional practices for using digital tools and resources in support of student learning.	regularly evaluate and reflect on current research and apply promising practices for using existing and emerging tools and resources in support of student learning.	contribute to the effective use of technology to enhance teaching and learning by conducting action research, evaluating the outcomes, and sharing the results locally and globally.
d. contribute to the effectiveness, vitality, and self-renewal of the teaching profession and of their school and community	identify strategies for contributing to the effectiveness, vitality, and self-renewal of the teaching profession and the school community.	demonstrate and discuss with colleagues the effective use of digital resources and related teaching and learning strategies to enhance student learning and the teaching profession.	actively contribute to the effectiveness, vitality, and self-renewal of the teaching profession by sharing promising practices for using technology to improve student learning with others in the school, profession, and community.	demonstrate, discuss, and present to parents, school leaders, and the larger community the impact on learning of the effective use of digital resources and the ongoing renewal of professional practice.

Scenario for Professional Growth & Leadership

5. Engage in Professional Growth and Leadership

Performance Indicator 5.a   Participate in local and global learning communities to explore creative applications of technology to improve student learning.

Other NETS Alignments   NETS•T 3.b

Proficient Level Rubric   Actively participate in local and global learning communities to exchange and implement ideas and methods related to creative applications of technology to improve student learning.

Teacher Simon Leung is no stranger to social networks. As a student, he had a Web presence on several online social networks. Now a classroom teacher, it was natural that Leung would look to online learning communities when he wanted ideas for classroom management and lesson planning.

"I'd hoped that my district might offer online mentoring," says Leung. "However, I discovered that this isn't something that's available yet." And so, Leung looked outside his district for assistance. "I didn't want online courses. I wanted to connect with fellow practitioners who could share ideas about the best way to set up a class project, or tips and tricks for home/school communication. Interactivity was a key requirement for me."

It took some searching to find the type of learning community he sought, but Leung finally discovered a social network that targets groups with a more professional focus. "Not only can I join existing networks related to education, but with a few clicks of a mouse button, I can create a new network for my own specific needs."

> ### Taking It to the Transformative Level
>
> *Help develop and sustain local and global learning communities to exchange ideas and methods related to creative applications of technology and to enhance the effective use of technology for learning.*
>
> *Now that he is familiar with learning communities outside his local area, Leung plans to propose that his district use online networking tools to create a local learning community for teachers at the district's 12 school sites. He is willing to help set up the group and make regular contributions to get it off the ground. "I know it will require extra time at first," he says, "but I think that many of my colleagues would find this kind of network extremely helpful."*

Once he made connections with other educators in this way, Leung learned that there are a variety of other sites where he could connect with educators from around the world—particularly those who were interested in finding creative ways to use technology to support student achievement. For example, he follows (and is followed by) a number of micro-blog users. Micro-blogs allow users to quickly share ideas and resources via short messages.

Recently, Leung set up an account in a popular multi-user virtual environment (MUVE), where he (actually his avatar) is now a regular attendee at education-related events. He can often be found on an education island in deep conversation with internationally known experts in curriculum and instruction. His explorations in MUVEs also led Leung to local and national professional organizations that provide member services including virtual and face-to-face workshops, conferences, and more.

As a result of his engagement in these online communities, Leung is learning about ways he can engage his students in similar online groups focused on service learning and cross-cultural projects. "I didn't realize so many good resources were available. I wish more of my colleagues were taking advantage of them."

NETS Project Overview

The Challenge

The challenge facing schools worldwide is to empower all students to function effectively now and in a future marked by increasing change, evolving technologies, and the phenomenal growth of information.

The Potential

Technology is a powerful tool with enormous potential for providing learning opportunities that will serve the needs of today's students throughout their lifetimes.

The Goal

Through the NETS Project, ISTE encourages educational leaders to use technology (ICT) standards to provide environments that enable students to use technology for improved learning. This includes assisting educational leaders in recognizing and addressing the essential conditions (see p. 3) for the effective use of technology in school settings.

The Results

ISTE released the first generation of the NETS•S (1998), NETS•T (2000), and NETS•A (2002) to wide acclaim and adoption. The original NETS created a roadmap for educational technology expectations for students across the U.S. and around the globe. In 2007, ISTE released the new NETS for Students, raising the bar on the quality and extent to which digital resources are used. The new NETS•S hold great promise for students of the digital age and bring to bear the higher order thinking skills future generations will need to make decisions, solve problems, create original works, and develop innovative ideas. The NETS Project has also provided teachers, technology planners, teacher preparation institutions, and educational decision makers with a wide variety of additional standards-based resources for establishing enriched learning environments supported by technology.

The Refresh Process

ISTE remains committed to tapping the collective wisdom of the global educational technology community for fresh and meaningful guidance and leadership. Thousands of education stakeholders from all 50 states in the U.S. and dozens of countries participated in the refresh of the NETS•S and the NETS•T. The process included open forum meetings at major education conferences and meetings; focus groups to collect input from education, business, and community organizations; virtual forum meetings; and online surveys. The ISTE Accreditation and Standards Committee compiled the responses and developed a draft that was reviewed and revised by the ISTE Stakeholders Advisory Council. The resulting draft of the refreshed NETS was then submitted for additional comments and suggestions online and in open forum meetings. The ISTE Board of Directors adopted the NETS•S on May 4, 2007, and the NETS•T on April 3, 2008.

Development Team

ISTE NETS Refresh Project Leadership Team

Lynn Nolan, NETS Refresh Director and Sr. Director of Education Leadership	*ISTE*
Lajeane Thomas, NETS Director	*Louisiana Tech University*
David Barr, Consultant	*ISTE*
Leslie S. Conery, Deputy CEO	*ISTE*
Mila M. Fuller, Director of Strategic Initiatives	*ISTE*
Don Knezek, CEO	*ISTE*
Anita McAnear, Acquisitions Editor	*ISTE*
Carolyn Sykora, Project Manager	*ISTE*

ISTE Accreditation and Standards Committee

Lajeane Thomas, Chair	*Louisiana Tech University*
Sheryl Abshire	*Calcasieu Parish Public Schools*
David Barr	*ISTE Consultant*
Jill Brown	*Albuquerque Academy*
Ann Cunningham	*Wake Forest University*
Kathy Hayden	*California State University San Marcos*
Paul Reinhart	*Conneaut Elementary School*
Heidi Rogers	*Northwest Council for Computer Education (NCCE)*
Steve Rainwater	*University of Texas at Tyler*

ISTE NETS Refresh Stakeholders Advisory Council

Jill Abbott	*Schools Interoperability Framework Association*
Stephen Andrews	*Intel® Education*
Barbara Cambridge	*National Council of Teachers of English*
Karen Cator	*Apple Inc.*
Anuja Dharkar	*Adobe Systems Inc.*
Alan Farstrup	*International Reading Association*
Christine Greenhow	*University of Minnesota*
Liz Hoffman	*American Council on the Teaching of Foreign Languages*
Margaret Honey	*Wireless Generation*
Sharnell Jackson	*Chicago Public Schools*
Peggy Kelly	*California State University San Marcos*
Paige Kuni	*Intel® Education*
Michal LeVasseur	*National Council for Geographic Education*
Tim Magner	*U.S. Department of Education*
Frank Owens	*National Science Teachers Association*
Andrea Prejean	*National Education Association*
Neal Strudler	*University of Nevada at Las Vegas*
Gayle Thieman	*National Council for Social Studies*
Jan Van Dam	*Pearson*
Carla Wade	*State Education Technology Directors Association*
Mary Ann Wolf	*State Education Technology Directors Association*

ISTE Board of Directors, 2007–2008

Trina Davis, President

Kurt Steinhaus, Past President

Helen Soulé, Executive Committee Treasurer and Corporate Representative

Helen Padgett, Executive Committee Secretary and Affiliate Representative

Camilla Gagliolo, Executive Committee At-Large Member and Special Interest Group Representative

Richard Martinez, Executive Committee At-Large Member and School District Administration Representative

Jeanne Biddle, At-Large Representative

Jill Brown, PK–12 Schools Representative

Deb deVries, Corporate Representative

Ryan Imbriale, Affiliate Representative

Doug Johnson, At-Large Representative

Ralph Leonard, International Representative

Howard Levin, At-Large Representative

Kyle Peck, Teacher Education Representative

Steve Rainwater, Computer Science Representative

Ferdi Serim, At-Large Representative

Carla Wade, State Technology Director Representative

Contributing Authors for This Booklet

Susan Brooks-Young

Jeff V. Bolkan

National Educational Technology Standards for Students products available from ISTE

"[A] groundbreaking paradigm for what young people should know about technology and what they should be able to do with it before graduating."—eSchool News

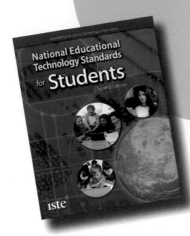

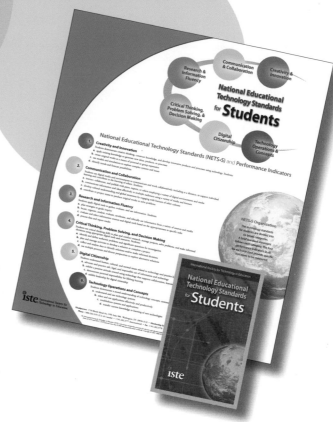

NETS•S Booklet
$12.95 ($9.05 ISTE members)
Product code NESBO2

NETS•S Poster
$9.95 ($6.95 ISTE members)
Product code NETSP3

NETS•S Brochure Pack—Pack of 25
$7.95 ($5.55 ISTE members)
Product code NETSU2

Look for the refreshed National Educational Technology Standards for Administrators in Summer 2009!